nsolved!

MYSTERIES OF THE COSMIC JOKER

Kathryn Walker

based on original text by Brian Innes

Crabtree Publishing Company

www.crabtreebooks.com

Crabtree Publishing Company

www.crabtreebooks.com

Author: Kathryn Walker
 based on original text by Brian Innes
Project editor: Kathryn Walker
Picture researcher: Rachel Tisdale
Managing editor: Miranda Smith
Art director: Jeni Child
Design manager: David Poole
Editorial director: Lindsey Lowe
Children's publisher: Anne O'Daly
Editor: Molly Aloian
Proofreader: Crystal Sikkens
Crabtree editorial director: Kathy Middleton
Production coordinator: Katherine Berti
Prepress technician: Katherine Berti

Cover: An artist's sketch showing a rain of frogs.
Some believe the cosmic joker is responsible for
the mysterious rainfalls of animals and objects.

Photographs:
Corbis: Canadian Museum of Civilization:
 p. 29; Leonard de Selva: front cover
Fortean Picture Library: p. 4
Istockphoto: Josu Altzelai: p. 27;
 Verena Matthew: p. 14
Mary Evans Picture Library: p. 11,
 12, 21
NOAA Photo Library: p. 13
Shutterstock: Elena Blokhina: p. 30;
 Entertainment Press: p. 9, 13, 19;
 Roxana Gonzalez: p. 25, 26; David
 Hughes: p. 5; LW Photography: p. 23;
 Ian Tragen: p. 8; Aaron Wood: p. 20
Topfoto: p. 7, 15, 17, 18, 22

Every effort has been made to trace the
owners of copyrighted material.

Library and Archives Canada Cataloguing in Publication

Walker, Kathryn, 1957-
 Mysteries of the cosmic joker / Kathryn Walker ; based
on original text by Brian Innes.

(Unsolved!)
Based on: Cosmic joker / Brian Innes.
Includes index.
ISBN 978-0-7787-4148-0 (bound).--ISBN 978-0-7787-4161-9 (pbk.)

 1. Fort, Charles, 1874-1932--Juvenile literature.
2. Science--Miscellanea--Juvenile literature. 3. Curiosities and wonders--
Juvenile literature. I. Title. II. Series: Unsolved! (St. Catharines, Ont.)

Q173.W34 2009   j001.94   C2009-902029-7

Library of Congress Cataloging-in-Publication Data

Walker, Kathryn.
 Mysteries of the cosmic joker / Kathryn Walker ; based on original text
by Brian Innes.
  p. cm. -- (Unsolved!)
 Includes index.
 ISBN 978-0-7787-4161-9 (pbk. : alk. paper) -- ISBN 978-0-7787-4148-0
(reinforced library binding : alk. paper)
 1. Science--Miscellanea--Juvenile literature. 2. Curiosities and wonders--
Miscellanea--Juvenile literature. 3. Fort, Charles, 1874-1932--Juvenile
literature. I. Innes, Brian. II. Title. III. Series.

Q173.W15 2010
001.94--dc22
                                          2009014155

Crabtree Publishing Company
www.crabtreebooks.com   1-800-387-7650

Published in Canada
Crabtree Publishing
616 Welland Ave.
St. Catharines, ON
L2M 5V6

Published in the United States
Crabtree Publishing
PMB16A
350 Fifth Ave., Suite 3308
New York, NY 10118

Published by CRABTREE PUBLISHING COMPANY in 2010

Contents

The Devil's Hoofmarks

...Some events seem impossible to explain.

On the morning of February 9, 1855, people in South Devon, England, woke to find strange prints in the freshly fallen snow. The prints looked like a donkey's hoofmarks. But a donkey would have left two lines of prints—these prints were in a single line.

The prints covered a distance of more than 100 miles (160 km). They ran through villages, along rooftops and high walls, and across fields. People wondered if they were the prints of some strange beast, or even the devil.

Over the centuries, there have been many other unexplained events. A man named Charles Hoy Fort spent his life studying these puzzling and sometimes humorous **occurrences**. He suggested they were the work of some mysterious force. This was how the idea of the **cosmic joker** was born.

>> **cosmic joker**—A power, or force, that causes various strange and unexplained happenings

The hoofmarks were about 8 inches (20 cm) apart, one behind the other.

It was suggested that the prints had been made by a rope trailing from an air balloon or even by jumping rats.

Some people think that wild animals could have made the prints. The weather may have caused the prints to change shape.

"...people in South Devon, England, woke to find strange prints in the freshly fallen snow."

The drawings on the left were made by someone who claimed to see the tracks found in the snow in February, 1855.

The World of Charles Fort

...Fort was fascinated by unexplained events.

Charles Fort was born in 1874 in Albany, New York. He was a writer who spent many years collecting details about strange events and trying to make sense of them.

Fort's first book on the subject—*The Book of The Damned*—went on sale in 1919. It is filled with reports of rainfalls of animals, stones, and other unusual objects. There are also stories of unknown flying objects, mysterious disappearances, and strange **coincidences**.

Fort found humor in a lot of the **bizarre** things that he wrote about. But he also found humor in some of the ways that scientists tried to explain the events. Fort was amazed at how scientists refused to believe anything that they could not explain.

How Strange...

∪ Charles Fort made thousands of notes on small squares of paper. After his death, more than 60,000 of these were left to the New York Public Library.

∪ Today, people often use the word "Fortean" to describe strange events.

>> **bizarre**—Extremely unusual or odd, often in an amusing way

This modern-day portrait of Charles Fort shows him surrounded by some of the things he wrote about—strange beasts and rainfalls of frogs.

Fort published three more books about mysterious occurrences. His last book—*Wild Talents*—appeared in 1932. In it, he suggests that some of these things are caused by the **extraordinary** powers of the human mind.

Fort's beliefs

Fort believed that everything is connected and that strange things happen for a reason. He said that the connections between things interested him more than the things themselves.

He also thought that space travel was possible. Fort made notes about unexplained lights and objects that people had seen in the sky. He was one of the first people to suggest that they might be spacecraft from other planets.

"Fort believed that everything is connected and that strange things happen for a reason."

Charles Fort wrote about strange objects in the sky. Today, we call these "unidentified flying objects" or UFOs.

>> **extraordinary**—Highly unusual or out of the ordinary

Fort thought that the force that had created the Rocky Mountains (pictured here) could also be the cause of many unexplained events.

Cosmic force

The word "teleportation" was invented by Fort. It means the movement of objects, people, or animals over distances by an unknown force. Fort believed that when the world was being formed, this same force—sometimes called cosmic force—caused mountains to form and continents to split. Then, as the force died down, it became the cause of more **mischievous** events, such as showers of fish or stones from the sky.

Fans of Fort

People still read Fort's books today and books have been written about him. In 1973, a magazine called *Fortean Times* was launched. It carries on the work of Charles Fort by reporting on strange events around the world.

How Strange...

- In 1884, two farmers in a field in Trenton, New Jersey, were hit by a shower of stones falling from the sky.

- Fort found humor in the idea that the same force that had formed the great Rocky Mountains might now be slinging stones at people in New Jersey.

>> **mischievous**—Full of mischief, or annoying in a playful way

Cosmic Jokes

...If there is a force that causes odd things to occur, maybe it has a sense of humor.

On February 20, 2006, villagers in the Kerala region of southwest India reported some very strange weather. The clouds burst and it began to rain fish! A local shop owner said: "At first, no one noticed it. But soon, we saw slushy objects on the ground and noticed some slight movement." People said the fish looked like parals, a common **freshwater** fish.

Stranger still, the village where the fishy rain fell was called Manna. In the Bible, "**manna**" is the name for food that falls down from heaven.

This story is not as unusual as you might think. Over the centuries, there have been many reports of rains of fish, frogs, and other animals. In December 1877, the *New York Times* reported that several young alligators had fallen on a farm in South Carolina. More recently, in April 1985, people claimed that starfish had fallen on parts of St. Cloud, Minnesota.

>> **freshwater**—From, or living in, water that is not salty

"...There have been many reports of rains of fish, frogs, and other animals."

This is an artist's idea of a rain of fish that was reported in 1859 in Mountain Ash, Wales. Supposedly, there were two showers. Each shower lasted for about two minutes.

Frog fall

In June 2005, thousands of tiny frogs fell from storm clouds over the town of Odzaci. This town is in Serbia, a country in southeastern Europe. The frogs were alive and hopping around. Locals said they were different from the frogs normally found in the area.

More heavy showers

Animals are not the only unusual things to suddenly fall out of the sky. On a clear day in March, 1876, it rained **flakes** of meat in Bath County, Kentucky. They turned out to be pieces of horse meat.

In December 1974, eggs began to fall from a clear sky in Wokingham, England. They crashed down on cars, fences, and on a school playground. Oddly, the name of the school was Keep Hatch. Some of the schoolchildren even picked up whole, unbroken eggs.

"Animals are not the only unusual things to suddenly fall out of the sky."

Boys from Keep Hatch School in Wokingham, England, hold up some of the eggs that fell from the sky in December 1974.

>> **flakes**—Flat, thin pieces

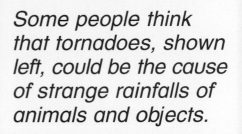

Some people think that tornadoes, shown left, could be the cause of strange rainfalls of animals and objects.

A possible explanation?

Scientists believe they can explain some of these strange rainfalls. They say that animals, and other objects can be sucked up into the air by **swirling** winds—known as whirlwinds or tornadoes. A tornado can also pull water up into the sky. This is called a waterspout.

When the wind drops, animals or objects that have been drawn up into these columns of air and water will fall to the ground. However, this does not explain why these strange rains often contain only one type of animal or object, such as corn husks, snakes, or frogs.

How Strange...

U In March 1977, it rained hazelnuts in a street in Bristol, England. There were no nut trees in the area, and it was not the time of year for nuts!

U A crop of unripe peaches fell on some workmen in Shreveport, Louisiana, in July 1961. The men said they came out of the sky.

Repeating pattern

There are some strange stories of people or families who have had the same unusual experience more than once. This happened to Joseph Figlock of Detroit.

In 1937, Figlock was sweeping an alley when a baby fell out of a fourth-story window and landed on him. Just one year later, Figlock was again hit by a baby falling from a fourth-story window in a different alley. Luckily, both babies survived the falls.

Double tragedy

Unfortunately, not all these stories end well. In 1975, a man in Bermuda was killed while riding his motorcycle. He was hit by a taxi.

One year later, the man's brother was killed in the same street while riding on the same motorcycle. Amazingly, both brothers were hit by the same taxi and it was being driven by the same person. The taxi was even carrying the same passenger.

> "Amazingly, both brothers were hit by the same taxi and it was being driven by the same person."

Bermuda (below) was the setting for two fatal accidents that were **eerily** similar.

>> **eerily**—Describing something strange and possibly frightening

Hand of fate

Carol Alspaugh lived in Grand Rapids, Michigan. Early in the morning of February 9, 1979, she spotted something odd. A large **icicle** was hanging outside her kitchen window. It was shaped like a human hand. Part of it was broken.

That day, Alspaugh's sister was going to have surgery on her hand. However, the doctors had to cancel the operation at the last minute because she injured her arm. This new injury had been caused by a falling icicle.

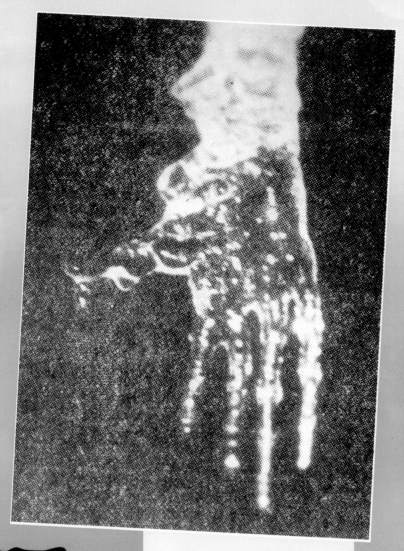

This is a photo of the handlike icicle that Carol Alspaugh saw on a February morning in 1979.

How Strange...

There are many cases of people with names that are strangely appropriate for the jobs at which they work. These include a weather person called Blizzard, a firearms store owner named Bang, and several doctors named Death.

More Than Chance?

...Some coincidences are so odd that they almost seem planned.

Everybody experiences coincidences at some time. For example, you might meet someone whose parents were born on the same day. But occasionally, coincidences are so weird that it seems as if some mischievous being has caused them to happen.

In 1898, American writer Morgan Robertson wrote a novel called *Futility*. It tells the story of a huge British **liner** called the *Titan*. One April night, the *Titan* hits an iceberg in the North Atlantic. It sinks, killing most of its crew and passengers.

In 1912, the British liner *Titanic* set off on its first voyage. One April night in the North Atlantic, it hit an iceberg and sank. Most of the people on board died—just as they did in Robertson's story.

>> **liner**—A large passenger ship or aircraft

How Strange...

- The **fictional** *Titan* and the real-life *Titanic* were traveling at similar speeds when they hit icebergs. Both were said to be traveling too fast.

- The ships were of similar size and both were built to carry about 3,000 passengers and crew.

This painting shows survivors escaping as the Titanic *sinks into freezing waters.*

>> **fictional**—Something that is not true but has been made up, as in a story

17

A kidnapping

A novel by Harrison James (his real name was James Rusk, Jr.) appeared in 1972. It tells the story of how a **terrorist** group kidnaps a woman named Patricia. Patricia was the daughter of a wealthy and famous man. At the end of the book, Patricia becomes a willing member of the terrorist gang. She has come to believe in the ideas they are fighting for.

On February 4, 1974, a young woman named Patricia, or Patty, Hearst was kidnapped by terrorists. She was the granddaughter of the wealthy newspaper owner, William Randolph Hearst. The FBI (Federal Bureau of Investigation) thought that this real-life event was so similar to the book that for a while they believed Rusk was involved.

Patty Hearst (center) is taken to court in handcuffs after taking part in a bank robbery.

There were more similarities to come. A few months later, Patty was photographed taking part in a bank robbery. She was later caught and sent to prison for helping the terrorists.

>> **terrorist**—Someone who uses violence as a political weapon

Lost and found

The Welsh actor Sir Anthony Hopkins has starred in many plays and movies. In 1971, he agreed to appear in a movie based on George Feifer's book *The Girl from Petrovka*. Hopkins traveled into London to buy a copy of the book, but failed to find one. He decided to return home.

At the subway station, Hopkins spotted a book lying on a bench. He could hardly believe his eyes—it was a copy of *The Girl from Petrovka*!

Two years later, Hopkins met George Feifer while he was filming. Feifer said he had no copies of his own book. He had lent his last one to a friend who had lost it. "Is this it?" asked Hopkins, handing Feifer the book he had found. Astonished, Feifer recognized **annotations** that he had made inside the book. It was his lost copy.

"...Hopkins spotted a book lying on a bench. He could hardly believe his eyes..."

Sir Anthony Hopkins once found himself part of a series of strange coincidences.

Coming home

Canadian actor, Charles Francis Coghlan died suddenly in 1899 while on tour in Galveston, Texas. He had to be buried in a Galveston cemetery because Coghlan's home was on Prince Edward Island, more than 3,000 miles (4,800 km) away by ship.

In September 1900, Galveston was destroyed by a **hurricane**. The graveyard was flooded and Coghlan's coffin floated out into the Gulf of Mexico.

Eight years later, some fishermen from Prince Edward Island spotted a coffin floating near the shore. Charles Coghlan's body had returned to its home! This time, he was buried in the cemetery of the church where he had been baptized.

This picture shows Prince Edward Island, where Charles Coghlan was finally laid to rest.

>> **hurricane**—A violent, tropical storm with a very strong wind

A double disaster

Amazing coincidences surround the life and death of King Umberto I of Italy. On July 28, 1900, Umberto dined at a restaurant in the town of Monza, Italy. He was surprised to discover that the restaurant owner looked exactly like him.

As the two men talked, they realized they had much more in common. Both were named Umberto. They had both been born in the city of Turin on March 14, 1844 and had both got married on the same day. Stranger still, each man had a wife named Margherita and a son who was named Vittorio.

On the following evening, King Umberto was informed that the restaurant owner had died in a shooting accident earlier in the day. Just as the king was saying how sorry he was, three shots rang out. King Umberto had been shot dead—on exactly the same date as his **double**.

"Amazing coincidences surround the life and death of King Umberto I of Italy."

King Umberto I of Italy, who was assassinated on July 29, 1900.

Fatal links

More than 100 years separate the **assassinations** of U.S. presidents Abraham Lincoln and John F. Kennedy. But many people believe that the two assassinations are linked by coinicidences.

Both men were shot in the back of the head on a Friday. Also, both were shot in front of their wives. John Wilkes Booth shot Lincoln in a theater, then hid in a barn. Lee Harvey Oswald shot Kennedy from a warehouse and hid in a movie theater.

Lincoln's secretary was named John Kennedy. He had warned Lincoln not to go to the theater that fateful evening. Kennedy's secretary was named Evelyn Lincoln. She had warned Kennedy not to go to Dallas, where he was shot. Both men were followed by a president named Johnson: Lincoln by Andrew Johnson, born 1808, and Kennedy by Lyndon Johnson, born 1908.

> "...many people believe that the two assassinations are linked..."

President John F. Kennedy is seen here (left) with his wife, just seconds before he was shot.

>> **assassination**—A murder carried out for political reasons

This railroad bridge is in Louisville, Kentucky. When George Bryson stopped off in the town, he got a big surprise.

More name games

There are many other strange coincidences involving people's names. For example, in the 1950s, a man named George D. Bryson was making a trip to New York City. As his train pulled in at Louisville, Kentucky, he suddenly decided to get off and visit the town.

Bryson made his way to a hotel, where he was given room 307. As a joke, he asked if there was any mail for him. To his surprise, there was a letter addressed to George D. Bryson, room 307. But it was not for him. The last **occupant** of room 307 had been another George D. Bryson.

How Strange...

In 1679, three men were hanged at Greenberry Hill, London for the murder of Sir Edmund Berry. The men's names were Green, Berry, and Hill.

In 1974, a man in Derby, England was listening to a recording of the song "Cry of the Wild Goose" when a Canadian goose crashed through his bedroom window.

>> **occupant**—Someone staying at or living in a particular place

Twin Tales

...There are some remarkable stories about twins.

About one-third of all twins are very similar. This means they have grown from the same egg and will look very much alike. Twins that are not **identical** have grown from two different eggs.

Most twins are raised together and have similar childhoods. They often seem to have a special way of understanding each other, without the need for words. But what about twins that are separated at birth and raised by different families?

The two Jims

Four-week-old twin boys were **adopted** by different families in Ohio in 1939. The twins first met when they were 39 years old. They discovered they had both been married twice, first to wives named Linda, then to wives named Betty. The men spoke and behaved the same way. Also, they were both named Jim!

How Strange...

 As children, both Jims owned dogs named Toy.

The two Jims had exactly the same health problems. They even used the same words to describe the headaches from which they both suffered.

>> **identical**—Exactly the same

"Twins...often seem to have a special way of understanding each other..."

Identical twins, such as the pair shown above, are always of the same sex and look very similar. It can be difficult to tell them apart.

Long-distance twins

Oskar Stohr and Jake Yufe were twins. They were born in 1933, in Trinidad in the West Indies. Their parents separated a few months after their birth. The boys were raised in different countries and with different beliefs.

Professor Thomas Bouchard of the University of Minnesota was doing **research** on identical twins that had been separated. In 1979, he arranged for Oskar and Jake to meet.

The twins arrived at the meeting both wearing blue shirts, wire-rimmed glasses, and identical mustaches. The men also shared many of the same habits, such as reading magazines from back to front and keeping rubber bands on their wrists. They both liked to startle people by sneezing very loudly in elevators!

"...They both liked to startle people by sneezing very loudly in elevators!"

Twins Oskar and Jake were both born on the island of Trinidad, but grew up in different parts of the world.

>> **research**—Study of a subject to find out new information about it

Sister story

English twins Barbara Herbert and Daphne Goodship were adopted by different families. They first met when they were 40. At their meeting, both were wearing cream dresses with brown velvet jackets.

The twins discovered they had a lot more in **common**. Both had met their husbands at a dance at age 16. Each had two sons, followed by a daughter. The twins shared a fear of heights and hated the sight of blood.

Startling similarity

It seems that even when twins are separated, something can cause their lives to follow the same pattern. In identical twins, this may be partly because they develop from the same egg. But can this explain all these similarities, or could the cosmic joker be at work here, too?

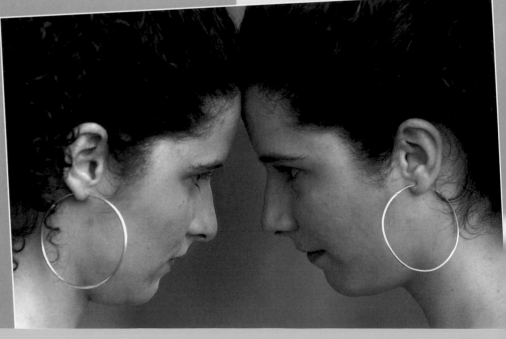

Making Sense

...Humans have always needed to make sense of strange events.

Long before Charles Fort, people around the world were looking for ways to understand unexplained occurrences. They invented a clever and mischievous being to blame. This character appears in many ancient **folktales** and legends. It loves to play tricks on the world, but is usually caught. People who study these stories call it the "**trickster**."

In Native American tales, the trickster is known as an animal, such as Raven or Coyote. In India and Africa, he often appears as Hare, while in China he is Monkey. The European trickster is usually a human who can turn into other shapes.

People everywhere notice how things do not always turn out the way they should. Tricksters represent the mysterious force or cosmic joker that makes the unexpected happen.

>> **folktale**—An old tale that is passed on by word of mouth

"In Native American tales, the trickster is known as an animal, such as Raven..."

This is a raven mask. The Native American peoples of the Pacific Coast of Canada have many tales about the trickster Raven.

>> **trickster**—A mischievous character in old tales who likes to play tricks and break rules

Scientists have recently become interested in the unexpected. Mathematicians are working on something called **chaos** theory. This may begin to explain what the cosmic joker really is.

Order in chaos

Some scientists are finding that different branches of math can predict things that happen in nature. The math also shows how the tiniest change in normal conditions can have a huge effect.

To give people an idea of what they mean, scientists use the following example: "A butterfly flaps its wings in an African forest and, not long after, a hurricane strikes the Florida coast." In other words, the breeze from a butterfly's wings could gather enough force to change the weather. The example also shows us how events that seem unconnected can actually have a huge effect on each other.

Charles Fort believed that all things are connected and that there is a reason for everything. Can science find out the reason for the events described in this book? Maybe one day the truth about the cosmic joker will be explained.

"Can science find out the reason for the events described in this book?"

The idea that something as small as the flapping of a butterfly's wings could make a huge difference has become known as the "butterfly effect."

>> **chaos**—Complete lack of order or organization

Glossary

adopted Taken in by a family to be raised as part of that family

annotation A comment or note explaining something

assassination A murder carried out for political reasons

bizarre Extremely unusual or odd, often in an amusing way

chaos Complete lack of order or organization

coincidence When two or more things happen separately, but seem to be connected

common Shared equally with another

cosmic joker A power, or force, that causes various strange and unexplained happenings

double Someone who looks exactly like someone else

eerily Describing something strange and possibly frightening

extraordinary Highly unusual or out of the ordinary

fictional Something that is not true but has been made up, as in a story

flakes Flat, thin pieces

folktale An old tale that is passed on by word of mouth

freshwater From, or living in, water that is not salty

hurricane A violent, tropical storm with a very strong wind

icicle A pointed stick of hanging ice formed from dripping water

identical Exactly the same

liner A large passenger ship or aircraft

manna In the Bible, food that falls from heaven.

mischievous Full of mischief, or annoying in a playful way

occupant Someone staying at or living in a particular place

occurrence Something that happens

research Study of a subject to find out new information about it

swirling Moving with a twisting or whirling motion

terrorist Someone who uses violence as a political weapon

trickster A mischievous character in old tales who likes to play tricks and break rules

Index

Further Reading

- Allen, Judy. *Unexplained: An Encyclopedia of Curious Phenomena, Strange Superstitions, and Ancient Mysteries.* Kingfisher, 2006.
- Barbo, Maria. *Creepy Stuff,* "Ripley's Believe It Or Not" series. Scholastic, 2002.
- Dennet, Preston. *UFOs and Aliens*, "Mysteries, Legends, and Unexplained Phenomena" series. Checkmark Books, 2008.
- Matthews, John & Caitlin. *Trick of the Tale: A Collection of Trickster Tales.* Candlewick, 2008.

Printed in the U.S.A.